HIP-HOP & R&B

Culture, Music & Storytelling

Alicia Keys

HIP-HOP & R&B

Culture, Music & Storytelling

Alicia Keys

Gucci Mane

Meek Mill

Migos

Beyoncé

Bruno Mars

Cardi B

Chance the Rapper

DJ Khaled

Drake

Jay-Z

John Legend

Lil Wayne

Nicki Minaj

Pharrell

Pitbull

Post Malone

Rihanna

The Weeknd

Travis Scott

Mason Crest
Carlie Lawson
HIP-HOP & R&B
Alicia Keys
Culture, Music & Storytelling

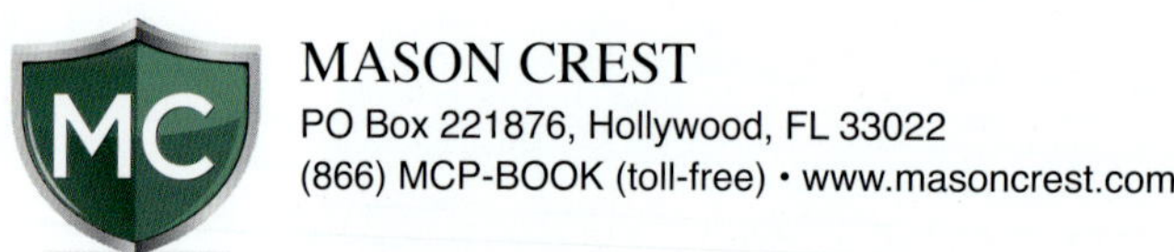

MASON CREST
PO Box 221876, Hollywood, FL 33022
(866) MCP-BOOK (toll-free) • www.masoncrest.com

Printed in the United States of America

First printing
9 8 7 6 5 4 3 2 1

ISBN (hardback) 978-1-4222-4626-9
ISBN (series) 978-1-4222-4625-2
ISBN (ebook) 978-1-4222-7186-5

Cataloging-in-Publication Data on file with the Library of Congress

Developed and produced by National Highlights Inc.
Editor: Regency House Publishing Ltd.
Cover Design: Annalisa Gumbrecht, Studio Gumbrecht

CONTENTS

KEY ICONS TO LOOK FOR:

Words to Understand: These words with their easy-to-understand definitions will increase the reader's understanding of the text while building vocabulary skills.

Sidebars: This boxed material within the main text allows readers to build knowledge, gain insights, explore possibilities, and broaden their perspectives by weaving together additional information to provide realistic and holistic perspectives.

Educational Videos: Readers can view videos by scanning our QR codes, providing them with additional educational content to supplement the text. Examples include news coverage, moments in history, speeches, iconic sports moments, and much more!

Text-Dependent Questions: These questions send the reader back to the text for more careful attention to the evidence presented there.

Research Projects: Readers are pointed toward areas of further inquiry connected to each chapter. Suggestions are provided for projects that encourage deeper research and analysis.

Series Glossary of Key Terms: This back-of-the-book glossary contains terminology used throughout this series. Words found here increase the reader's ability to read and comprehend higher-level books and articles in this field.

Alicia Keys
HIP-HOP & R&B

Chapter 1

Career Highlights—
Setting Recording Industry Records

Alicia Keys debuted as a honey-faced teen with long braids and slick lyrics. With a lilt in her voice and a tilt in her hips, she romanced listeners with her penchant for "Fallin,'" in and out of love.

The record companies might have stuttered, but listeners saw and heard her superstar future. Her initial record company couldn't hear the hits among her tracks. Columbia executives called her songs for what was to be her first album a "very

Alicia Keys on stage for a Good Morning America concert at the Rockefeller Center, New York City in 2007.

Scan to watch the video for Alicia Keys's breakthrough hit "Fallin.'"

long demo." They couldn't hear the Grammys in her classical- and jazz-influenced compositions.

Keys moved to Arista, drawn by her association with the Robinson brothers, one of whom scouted new talent for the label. "Fallin,'" one of the insulted demo songs, went number one for six weeks on the Billboard Hot 100.

Her orchestral arrangements and layered vocals appeal to a listening public that favors crossovers. Since her 2001 debut album, Keys has earned 15 Grammy Awards, sold more than 35 million albums, and penned hits for herself and others. She has now authored her first book and returned to acting.

Keys often collaborates with rap and hip-hop legends like Kanye West and Usher. West produced her hit "You Don't Know My Name." Her collaboration with Usher, "My Boo," held the number-one Hot 100 position for six weeks. Her second album, which featured both songs, also won her four Grammys.

In 2007, Keys delved into experimental pop with the album *As I Am*, then shifted to downbeat R&B jams with 2009's *The Element of Freedom*. Keys merged the two sounds for a sophisticated mix of the sounds on 2012's *Girl on Fire*.

Her pop experimentation coincided with her 2007 theatrical debut. She appeared in the film *Smokin' Aces*, with co-stars Ben Affleck and Ryan Reynolds. She followed it up with roles in *The Secret*

Alicia Keys   HIP-HOP & R&B

Life of Bees and *The Nanny Diaries.* The singer branched out to television as well, appearing on *Empire*. Since her brief stint with Columbia, Keys has released seven box sets, six studio albums, two live albums and one remix album. Her career has included 32 singles and two promotional singles. That does not include the plethora of works she has recorded with other artists for their projects. Worldwide, she has sold more than 42 million albums. In late November of 2019, she released a single, "Time Machine," without revealing whether it indicated a new album in the works or whether she was pulling a Prince and releasing an online only song.

All Released Solo Albums to Date:
Discography

SONGS IN A MINOR
(Released June 5, 2001)

Keys released her debut album in 2001. It charted at number one on the Billboard 200 and sold 236,000 units in its first week. *Songs in A Minor* prompted Keys's first headlining tour. The critics loved the tracks on it, and Keys won her first five Grammy Awards based on the album. It also became an instant classic, and in 2013, *Entertainment Weekly* named the album to its greatest albums of all-time list, placing it at number 57.

Alicia Keys arriving at the 11th Annual BET Awards at the Shrine Auditorium, Los Angeles in 2004.

THE DIARY OF ALICIA KEYS
(Released December 2, 2003)

Her follow-up album hit the U.S. Billboard 200 chart at number one with a bullet. The phrase "number one with a bullet" refers to an album or song that takes the top slot on the charts without first entering at a lower rank and climbing to number one. It sold 618,000 copies in its first week. The album produced three top-ten singles in the U.S. Most critics lauded *The Diary of Alicia Keys* as well, while record sales combined with industry respect helped it earn the musician three additional Grammy Awards. It ranks as the 31st best-selling album of the 2000s with U.S. sales of four million copies and sales of eight million copies worldwide.

AS I AM
(Released November 9, 2007)

Keys's third release also hit the U.S. Billboard 200 chart at number one with a bullet. It sold nearly three-quarters of a million units in its first week—742,000 copies. No other female R&B artist has achieved such high numbers. As time passed, the album's sales earned the Recording Industry Association of America's (RIAA) triple-platinum status. Selling well worldwide, the release produced four chart singles. One of those singles—"No One"—became 2007's most listened-to song in the U.S. While some critics panned her

Alicia Keys attending the *Glory Road* film premiere at Pantages Theatre, Los Angeles in 2006.

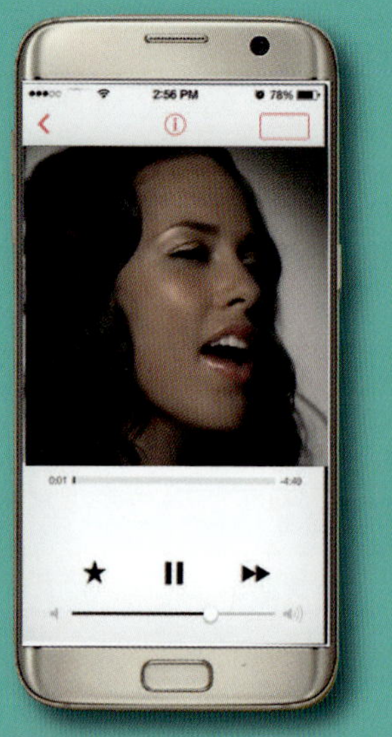

Scan here to watch the music video for Alicia Keys's "Superwoman."

songwriting, overall the album received positive reviews. Critical acclaim combined with worldwide sales of five million copies led to three more Grammy Awards. Outside North America, on November 10, 2008, *As I Am* was reissued in super edition with three added selections which included her collaboration with Jack White for the soundtrack of *Quantum of Solace*. The super edition also includes a second disc of five performances recorded at The Coronet in London.

THE ELEMENT OF FREEDOM
(Released December 11, 2009)

The Element of Freedom became Keys's first number-one album in the UK. It debuted at number two in the U.S. with first-week sales of 417,000. Within its first month of release, it earned platinum status from the Recording Industry Association of America (RIAA). The album produced five chart singles plus positive reviews. Critics complimented its low-key style and the cohesive nature of the release. Initially, Canadian rapper Drake was to write one song with Keys for the album, but the two jelled so well together that after writing "Un-thinkable (I'm Ready)," they simply kept going. Drake ended up contributing in some way to the entirety of the songs on the album. *The Element of Freedom* sold more than four million copies by August 2012, becoming the 148th bestselling release of the 2010s.

Alicia Keys HIP-HOP & R&B

Collaborations

- "Un-thinkable (I'm Ready) [Remix]," featuring Drake
- "Put It in a Love Song," featuring Beyoncé Knowles

GIRL ON FIRE

(Released November 22, 2012)

Although its title song has become an anthem of accomplished women everywhere and of young women on their way up, the album *Girl on Fire* had the lowest opening-week sales of any Keys album. It still debuted at number one though, selling 159,000 copies in the first week. The song "Girl on Fire" hit number two on the Hot R&B/Hip-Hop Song chart. It reached number eleven on the Billboard Hot 100. The women's success anthem hit

Scan here to watch the music video for Alicia Keys's "Girl on Fire."

Alicia Keys performs in concert at the American Airlines Arena, Miami in 2010.

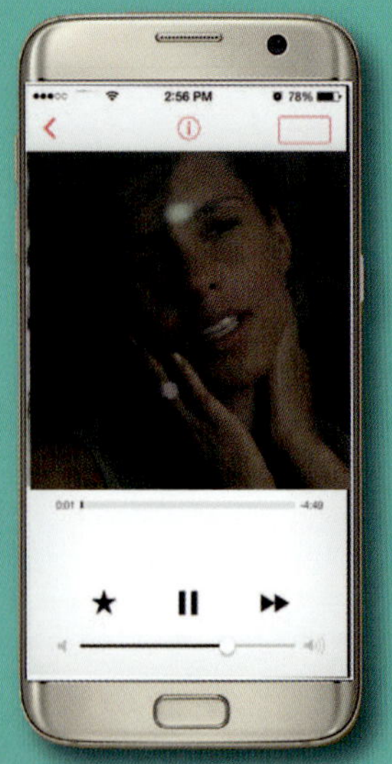

Scan here to watch the music video for Alicia Keys's "Tears Always Win."

Nicki Minaj collaborated with Alicia Keys on the Inferno Version of her famous hit "Girl on Fire."

the Top-ten charts in numerous countries. *Girl on Fire* also spawned three urban contemporary singles, "Brand New Me," "New Day," and "Fire We Make," a collaboration with Maxwell. At that year's Grammys, the album placed Keys in a rare category—the most awarded artist in a category. She won the Grammy for Best R&B Album for the third time. *Girl on Fire* has sold 1.1 million copies in the United States.

Collaborations

- "Girl on Fire [Inferno Version]," featuring Nicki Minaj
- "Fire We Make," featuring Maxwell

Here

(Released November 4, 2016)

Keys largely wrote *Here* in 2014 but put the album on hold when she learned she was

Alicia Keys   HIP-HOP & R&B

pregnant. In 2016, she recorded the album at Jungle City Studios and Oven Studios in New York, working with her husband, Swizz Beatz, and his colleagues Mark Batson, Illangelo, Jimmy Napes, and Pharrell Williams. *Here* debuted at number two on the U.S. Billboard 200 and topped Top R&B/Hip-Hop Albums chart, her seventh release to do so. The topical album explored African American life and social issues. It has sold 131,000 copies worldwide and received critical acclaim for its musical quality and issue-oriented tracks.

ALICIA
(Released September 18, 2020)

This is the seventh studio album recorded and largely written and produced by Keys. It was released by RCA Records. The album was a critical success, with reviewers applauding her vocal performances and the balanced quality of the lyrics.

UNPLUGGED
(Released October 7, 2005)

Keys released her first live album in 2005, in partnership with the MTV's program *Unplugged*. She performed her biggest hits at the time for a small audience at the Brooklyn Academy of Music in Brooklyn, New York City. Containing live, acoustic versions of hits from *Songs in A Minor* and *The Diary of Alicia Keys*, it hit the U.S. Billboard 200

Alicia Keys attends the Keep A Child Alive Black Ball at the Hammerstein Ballroom with her husband, Swizz Beatz on September 30, 2010 in New York City.

Scan the code to watch Alicia Keys's "Put It In A Love Song" featuring Beyoncé.

chart at number one with a bullet, selling 196,000 copies in its initial week of release. The album became the first *Unplugged* release from a female artist to debut at the top of the chart. It sold more than 2.5 million copies worldwide. The album spawned two singles, "Unbreakable," which reached number thirty-four on the U.S. Billboard Hot 100, and "Every Little Bit Hurts."

VH-1 STORYTELLERS
(Released October 28, 2008)

Keys released a second live album in partnership with the MTV brand. This one was for its VH-1 *Storytellers* series, a television program on one of its sister stations. While the artist performed hits like "No One" and "You Don't Know My Name," she also introduced new music from the *Girl on Fire* album, like "Brand New Me" and "Not Even the King" years before they would hit a studio album. Consistent with the TV show's format, she told the stories behind each song.

Other Collaborations

- "Empire State of Mind featuring Alicia Keys," JAY-Z from *The Blueprint 3*, 2009
- "Calma (Alicia Remix)," Pedro Capó, Alicia Keys and Farruko from *Calmai*, 2018
- "Gangsta Lovin'," featuring Alicia Keys and Eve from *Eve-olution*, 2002
- "Another Way to Die," Alicia Keys and Jack White

Alicia Keys at the 2009 BET Awards at the Shrine
Auditorium, Los Angeles in 2009.

- from *The Best of Bond ... James Bond,* 1992
- "Warrior Song," Nas featuring Alicia Keys from *The Warrior Song,* 2009
- "Ghetto Story Chapter 2," Cham featuring Alicia Keys, online release, 2006
- "Looking for Paradise," Alejandro Sanz featuring Alicia Keys from *Paraíso Express,* 2009
- "Know Who You Are," Pharrell Williams with Alicia Keys from *GIRL,* 2014
- "My Boo," Usher and Alicia Keys from *Confessions,* 2004
- "Lesson Learned," featuring John Mayer and Alicia Keys from *As I Am,* 2007
- "Mr. Man," Jimmy Cozier and Alicia Keys from *Songs in A Minor,* 2001
- "Fireworks," featuring Alicia Keys and Drake from *Thank Me Later,* 2010

The Inside Skinny on Some Major Collaborations

With each album and performance Alicia Keys illustrates her love of music. She explores the diversity genres and collaborates with a wide variety of musicians and rappers in an effort to explore new horizons. Her frequent collaborators include Kanye West, Drake,

Alicia Keys has collaborated with Kanye West several times.

and her producer husband, Swizz
Beatz.

"Un-thinkable (I'm Ready)"
by Drake, performed by Alicia
Keys, produced by Alicia Keys
(Released 2009)

"She gave me one of the best
studio experiences of my life, and
instead of being like 'Here's the beat.
Come on and get to work,' she said,
'Play me your favorite songs and we'll
battle.' It turned into this . . . heated
party, and we were just loving music. . . .
She didn't even play the keys and just
started writing melodies, and we came
up with the song. And I wrote most of
the record, and she produced it."

—Drake on working with Alicia Keys
on the album *The Element of Feeling.*

Empire State of Mind
with JAY-Z
(Performed 2009)

"The feeling I had being on stage with her and
Jay is beyond words in the dictionary. I couldn't
believe it. It was so Rat Pack. . . . Alicia keys helped
to make it epic."

Alicia Keys worked with
Drake on "Un-thinkable
(I'm Ready)."

—Nas, on working with Alicia Keys and JAY-Z on
the debut New York City performance of "Empire
State of Mind."

Alicia Keys HIP-HOP & R&B

No One *performed by Aretha Franklin, arranged by Alicia Keys*
(Released 2014)

"Alicia [Keys], of course, is a label mate, and it was her idea to put that reggae flavor on "No One." I thought that was just great, right on the money."

—Aretha Franklin on brainstorming song ideas with Keys for her album *Aretha Franklin Sings the Great Diva Classics*.

Tours Completed

Alicia Keys has completed five major tours of her own as headliner.

THE *SONGS IN A MINOR* TOUR

The tour spanned a year and seven months, beginning on January 10, 2001, and ending on August 30, 2002. It included 58 dates and was her first headlining tour.

THE *VERIZON LADIES FIRST* TOUR

Keys hit the road again in 2004 in North America to support her sophomore studio effort, *The Diary of Alicia Keys*. She shared headlining duties with singers Beyoncé, Missy Elliott, and Tamia for the 25-date tour.

Scan the code to watch Alicia Keys's "Girlfriend."

Scan here to watch the video for the Alicia Keys "Show Me Love" ft. 21 Savage and Miguel.

THE *DIARY* TOUR

The artist also embarked on her own headlining tour in support of her sophomore studio release, *The Diary of Alicia Keys*. The 36-date tour kicked off on February 28, 2005.

THE *AS I AM WORLD* TOUR

Her *As I Am* tour took Keys across the globe in support of her third studio release. It launched in February of 2008 and included 94 dates in a plethora of countries. Its final date was performed on December 20, 2008, in Australia.

THE *FREEDOM WORLD* TOUR

Keys also mounted a world tour in 2010 in support of her fourth studio album, *The Element of Freedom*. Keys sandwiched 50 dates into the tiny period from February 26, 2010, to June 10, 2010, a departure from her typical tour schedule, which spread dates out over a extended period of time. She began in North America and ended in South Africa.

THE *SET THE WORLD ON FIRE WORLD* TOUR

Keys launched the world tour to support *Girl on Fire* on March 7, 2013, in North America. Ending December 19, 2013, in New Zealand, the tour became Keys's last to date.

Other Performances

Keys performed scattered dates of stand-alone shows to support *Here*. She has limited live performances since becoming a mother.

Words to Understand

Disillusioned: Expressing disappointment when one discovers a person or thing to be less good than previously thought or believed.

Melodrama: A dramatic book, play, or moving picture with sensationalized, over-exaggerated characters and magnified life events that illicit emotional audience responses.

Speculation: Conjecture or the formation of a theory without actual facts or firm evidence.

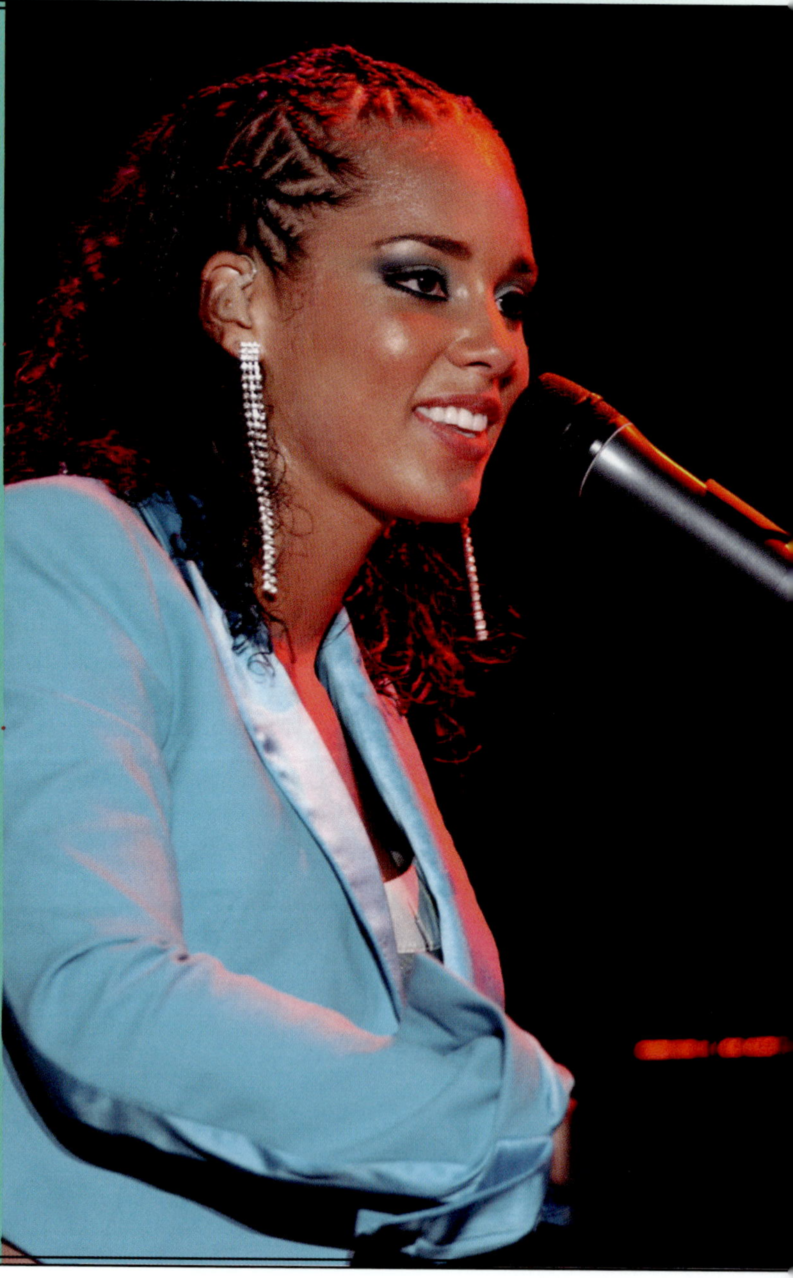

Alicia Keys in concert at the Cornetto Free Music Festival in Milan, Italy.

The Road to the Top— Fulfilling a Lifelong Dream

Alicia Keys, born Alicia Augello Cook, carved out multiple careers as an actress, author, musician, professional singer, and record producer. Her contributions to rhythm and blues (R&B) began in the 1990s and have culminated in her winning twelve Grammy Awards so far, as well as a number of American Music Awards and Billboard Awards. Keys won five of those Grammys in a single year, which ties her with Amy Winehouse and Lauryn Hill for the most Grammys won by a woman in a single year. In addition to critical acclaim, fans gobble up her music. *Songs in A Minor*, her debut, sold more than 12 million copies.

Alicia Keys arrives at the MTV Video Music Awards on August 29, 2004 in Miami.

Hell's Kitchen Beginnings

Born January 25, 1981, to Teresa Augello and Craig Cook, Keys's mother gained custody when the couple divorced in 1983. Augello and her daughter lived in the Hell's Kitchen area of New York City. Augello provided for the family by working as a paralegal and an actress, while Cook contributed to the household through his career as a flight attendant. Her multi-career mom worked by day at the law

Gang Violence—The neighborhood in which Keys grew up represents a growing problem in U.S. cities, which play host to more than 27,000 gangs spread across the nation, according to the National Gang Center. From 1996 to 2003, gang membership had been declining in the U.S., but a resurgence began in 2012, and gangs have seen an uptick in growth. Once the purview of major cities like New York City and Los Angeles, gangs have moved into all larger U.S. cities and many suburban areas. These locations account for about two-thirds of the U.S. gang members. Smaller cities host about 27 percent of gang members, and rural counties remain relatively peaceful. A little more than five percent of gang membership resides in rural areas.

firm of Chadbourne & Parke at Rockefeller Center from 1980 to 2001. After her 9-to-5 hours, she worked as an actress and helped her daughter get her start in acting, too.

Keys draws her unique beauty from her Italian-American mother and her Jamaican father. Fans first saw her at age four, when she appeared in an episode of the *The Cosby Show*. Keys's mother recognized her daughter's talent and potential early on and enrolled her in piano, gymnastics, art, theater, and dance lessons starting at age seven. Piano resounded with her the most, and she focused on that.

As an adult, Keys regards the focus on music as the catalyst for keeping her away from gangs. She carried a homemade knife to keep herself safer while going between school and her afterschool lessons. Unlike the roughness of the neighborhood, her piano studies provided a refined respite to her childhood. Her classical music studies exposed her to Beethoven, Chopin, and Mozart, with Chopin becoming her favorite composer.

Alicia Keys grew up in Hell's Kitchen, an area of Manhattan, New York City.

Five years into her studies, Keys began composing music. Appreciating her twelve-year-old daughter's songwriting talent, Teresa enrolled her in the city's Professional Performing Arts School. The school focused on choral music but also taught R&B. There, her classical music exposure expanded to include established blues performers and composers Billie Holiday, Duke Ellington, and Miles Davis as well as the R&B work of Stevie Wonder.

During high school, Keys studied under Aziza Miller whom she describes as "one of the most phenomenal women jazz instructors ever to be born." Keys says of the "badass" arranger, composer, pianist, producer, and vocalist. "I know for a fact that she influenced a large part of what I became."

Scan here to watch the video for the Alicia Keys video "Blended Family."

High-School Breakthrough

Since Keys's mom worked as an actress when she was growing up, it came as no surprise that Keys also went into acting. Her first career began at the age of four with an appearance on *The Cosby Show* that her mom helped her land. Both women went on auditions, and Keys's mom ensured that she benefitted from a well-rounded creative education.

At 14, she expanded her piano studies to jazz and formed a three-girl group called EmBishion. The band performed in Harlem. Her

Alicia Keys attended the Professional Performing Arts School in New York City where she discovered R&B through the music of Stevie Wonder.

vocals caught the ear of voice coach Conrad Robinson who introduced her to his brother R&B manager Jeff Robinson. The Robinson brothers auditioned her and expressed awe at her compositions and lyrics. She so impressed Jeff Robinson that he became her long-time manager. He helped her land her first professional record contract at fifteen with Columbia Records. She graduated high school the following year, at age sixteen, matriculating at Columbia University on a full scholarship. Her college days lasted only four weeks, because she stayed slammed with recording commitments. It was during that month of college that she wrote and collaborated on the hit song "Dah Dee Dah (Sexy Thing)."

Her time at neither Columbia lasted long though. The record company provided no creative freedom and wanted radio ready tunes. Producers called her compositions a "very long demo." The chart toppers that the record company promised did not come.

Alicia Keys attended Columbia University in New York City on a full scholarship.

Disillusioned, she rented her own apartment, lived alone, and worked on her music. She purchased recording equipment and cut demos at home. An introduction to Clive Davis led to a new contract with Arista Records. His retirement and the founding of his own the record label J Records prompted Keys to move to J Records.

Sweet 16 also became the year a friend introduced Keys to a young producer who was a year older. She became friends with Kasseem Dean, better known as Swizz Beatz. Now husband and wife, the couple took years to date, and they kept the relationship secret for a long time. Keys only alluded to her boyfriend in an interview with Oprah. Dean was still married to his ex-wife at the time. The songstress described the **melodrama** that unfolded when she and Dean finally went public in the song "Blended Family (What You Do for Love)," in which she directly addressed how the press wounded her step-children with its coverage of the relationship and endless **speculation**.

Swizz Beats and Alicia Keys keep their relationship secret for many years.

Alicia Keys

Alicia Keys is heavily involved in politics and has campaigned with Hillary Clinton.

"I know it started with a little drama/ I hate you had to read it in the paper/ But everything's alright with me and your momma."

Keys had two children with Dean, and he had children from prior relationships—a son, Prince Nasir, with Nicole Levy, a son, Kasseem Jr., with songwriter Mashonda Tifrere, and a girl, Nicole, with Jahna Sebastian. Dean and Keys married in 2010.

Feminism and the Women's Movement

Keys supports other women in their goal-setting and achievement. She wrote "Girl on Fire" in reference to herself and the larger group of young women of today. This feminism has led her to high level involvement in politics. She actively campaigned for Hillary Clinton in 2016. She regularly participates in protest marches and political rallies, using her celebrity status to shine the light on today's issues, especially those affecting the African American community and impoverished areas.

Keys often weaves her true-life experiences into her music. She described to *The Guardian* her upbringing in Hell's Kitchen and how it influenced her music and her attitudes: "These are the streets that I walked, and learned my lessons on, and heard the music, and witnessed disenfranchised people, and people who just had dreams and hopes. Every pimp, every prostitute, every drug dealer, every Broadway dreamer wishing they could be a writer, or a musician, or an actor."

Becoming Alicia Keys

Following the birth of her two children, Egypt Daoud Dean and Genesis Ali Dean, Keys put touring on hold. While she has continued

Alicia Keys and her son Egypt Daoud Dean.

Alicia Keys at the KIIS FM's Jingle Ball in 2012, held at the Nokia Theatre in Los Angeles.

working with other artists, she has not yet released another album since *Here.* She had already written all of the material for that record in 2014. The songwriter put its release on hold to focus on her pregnancy and the birth of her second child.

Keys parents a larger brood though. She co-parents all of her husband's children. That means her mom duties include raising children from kindergarten through high-school age. Their blended family of five children keeps both busy. Keys has focused less on touring and more on business interests, philanthropy, and writing her first book. These projects have allowed her to spend more time being a mother during her children's most formative years.

Text-Dependent Questions:

1. With what girl group did Alicia Keys perform in high school?

2. What music producer did Keys marry, and who are their mutual frequent collaborators?

3. What achievement did Keys become the first woman to earn?

Research Project:

Keys became part of a blended family when she married Dean. How common are blended families in the U.S. and in the world? What are some of the challenges faced by blended families?

Authenticity: The quality of being or genuine.

Creative director: The person at a company, such as an advertising agency, who leads the advertising and marketing of the company and manages the design and sales teams and marketers in creative visioning.

Autobiography: A self-authored story of a person's life.

Alicia Keys stopped wearing makeup in a bid to empower women to embrace their natural beauty.

Alicia Keys HIP-HOP & R&B

Chapter 3

Alicia Keys's Hip-Hop Career, Interests, and Passions in Moments

More Than Just a Musician

Alicia Keys maintains careers in acting, writing, music, and business. She has founded two non-profit organizations to tackle education issues that are important to her. She has played a bit part on *Charmed*, guest-starred on the television shows *Empire, American Dreams*, and *The Backyardigans* and has appeared in the films *Smokin' Aces, The Nanny Diaries, The Secret Life of Bees*, and *Jem and the Holigrams*. She also acted in two short films in 2019—*The Hamilton Mixtape* and *Let Me In*. She frequently appears in the videos for other artists, including the recent video for "Calma."

The Multi-Career Life

Keys, a multi-career woman, does not limit herself. She started acting professionally at age four and continues to enjoy working as

Alicia Keys performing at the 2016 UEFA Champions League soccer final in Milan, Italy.

Alicia Keys starred in *The Secret Life of Bees* an adaptation of a novel by Sue Monk Kidd.

an actress. The smattering of above titles represents only a smattering of the 54 acting credits she has amassed. Although many are song videos of her own and other artists', she also has appeared in numerous short films, TV shows and feature films. Her biggest part so far has been as June Boatwright in *The Secret Life of Bees*. She has appeared as herself on shows including CBS Good Morning and Jimmy Kimmel Live as well as talent shows like *The Voice* and *The X Factor: Celebrity*. Keys has also contributed songs to 176 TV and film soundtracks. Keys's appearances as herself in TV and movies number 268, including the upcoming documentary *I Talk to Strangers*. She directed and produced the television show "Five" on Lifetime, the Broadway show, "Stick Fly," and the feature films "The Inevitable Defeat of Mister & Pete."

Alicia Keys attended the Billboard Women In Music event held at the Hollywood Palladium, Los Angeles in 2019.

Oprah Winfrey endorsed Alicia Keys's book by allowing her to publish under her publishing imprint.

In 2019, Keys released her first book, *More Myself: A Journey*, which was the first title to come out on Oprah's publishing imprint. When she announced it, she gave props to Lady O.

"Thank you, Ms. O, for the opportunity to share my truth as the first release of your new book imprint," Keys stated on YouTube. "Our journeys are beautifully woven together and our messages are similar: now, more than ever, it's time to continue to honor ourselves by walking more unrelentingly in our **authenticity**, no matter what!"

Keys chose to refer to the **autobiography** as a journey rather than a memoir. It is less a story of her life (so far) than a treatise on a young woman of the twenty-first-century developing her identity. The

Women with Multiple Careers—Alicia Keys works at multiple careers, including musician, actress, former creative director of BlackBerry, author, and philanthropist. She is also a mother of two who co-parents her husband's three children from previous relationships. She represents one of the millions of Americans who work two or more jobs.

songwriter speaks openly about her journey of self-identity and exudes confidence in her authentic self.

"We want to be kind and loving to each other of course, but the goal is making yourself happy," Keys says. "That you are learning more about yourself. That you are able to identify more about who you are. What you like, what you love, what makes you feel magic."

You could argue that Alicia Keys's popularity stems from her authenticity as much as from her talent. While all performers have a marketing team and slant, Keys remains a down-to-earth individual who seems quite Everywoman. She wears no makeup. She mothers her blended brood of five. She cut back her work hours when her two children were born. She favors natural hairstyles.

Her music contains that same rare honesty as her image. She song writes on piano and favors songs that can easily sound as beautiful stripped down as lushly layered on a studio album. Her vocal range of three-octaves-plus-a-little provides plenty of range for pop and R&B.

Endorsements

Keys eschews most of the "deals" that many other performers pursue. Some artists willingly lend their name to brand after brand, but Keys limits the number and types of products she represents. In 2008, she had a cigarette company pulled as a sponsor for one of her concerts in Jakarta, Indonesia. She had seen promotional posters for the concert, which prominently showed an advertisement for Mild cigarettes, a Phillip Morris brand. Keys does not smoke and does not advocate doing so. In line with her authenticity, she sent a message to her record company to have it remove the sponsor from the posters.

When Keys does partner with a brand, she genuinely feels that it matches her values and would not hurt her fans. To date, she has only had two major brand partnerships, Levi's and Blackberry.

Levi's

Keys partnered with denim company Levi's in 2015 to launch its women's denim collection. She served as a global brand representative for the campaign. Called "Live in Levi's," Keys provided the soundtrack for the ad campaign with the song "28,000 Days." She represented the brand as a spokesperson and style icon.

Scan here to watch an interview with Alicia Keys, in which she discusses her book, *More Myself*.

Alicia Keys — HIP-HOP & R&B

"When you are authentically yourself, you are so gorgeous and powerful. I've come to the revelation that I'm just a jeans girl at heart. I feel the most confident, comfortable, sexy, and strong in my jeans," Keys said in an interview with *Branding Forum*. "Levi's is for every woman … there is something for everyone … much like music, Levi's brings people together from all walks of life and cultures."

Keys appeared in the company's digital and social platform posts and TV, cinema, and print advertisements. "Alicia Keys embodies that spirit of the brand and brings it to life in such an inspiring and resonant way for women everywhere," said Levi's chief marketing officer, Jen Sey.

BLACKBERRY

BlackBerry, formerly known as Research in Motion (RIM), contracted with Keys in 2013 to represent the BlackBerry smartphone when it released it. The Z10 marked the first release of a smartphone for the company, whose market share had been overtaken by Android and iPhones. BlackBerry did not hire Keys as a brand representative though. Rather, it hired her as its new global **creative director**.

The singer switched gears from making music to making business decisions. Her position involved activities that would lead to "new business initiatives that will drive engagement with BlackBerry." Her work centered on the Z10, developed after the firm's marketing

Awards Won

Alicia Keys has won a bevy of accolades for vocal performance, production, and songwriting. She has racked up an impressive number of Grammys and AMA awards for her albums and collaborations.

American Music Awards (AMAs)

Favorite Soul/R&B Album for *As I Am* | Won in 2008

Favorite Pop/Rock Album for *As I Am* | Won in 2008

Favorite Soul/R&B Female Artist | Won in 2004

Favorite Soul/R&B New Artist | Won in 2002

Favorite Pop/Rock New Artist | Won in 2002

BET Awards

Best Collaboration, Duo or Group for *"Empire State of Mind"* | Won in 2010

Best Hip-Hop Video for *"Empire State of Mind"* | Won in 2010

Best Female R&B/Pop Artist | Won in 2010

Best Collaboration for *"Empire State of Mind"* | Won in 2010

BET Humanitarian Award | Won in 2009

Best Female R&B/Pop Artist | Won in 2005

Best Female R&B/Pop Artist | Won in 2008

Best New Artist | Won in 2002

Echo Award

Best International Newcomer for *Songs in A Minor* | Won in 2002

Grammy Awards

Best Rap Song for *"Empire State of Mind"* (Songwriters) | Won in 2010

Best Rap/Sung Collaboration for *"Empire State of Mind"* | Won in 2010

Best Female R&B Vocal Performance for *"Superwoman"* (Artist) | Won in 2008

Best Female R&B Vocal Performance for *"No One"* | Won in 2007

Best R&B Song for *"No One"* | Won in 2007

Best R&B Album for *The Diary of Alicia Keys* (Artist, Engineers/Mixers) | Won in 2004

Best R&B Song for *"You Don't Know My Name"* (Songwriters) | Won in 2004

Best R&B Performance by a Duo or Group with Vocals for *"My Boo"*
(feat. Alicia Keys) (Artists) | Won in 2004

Best Female R&B Vocal Performance for *"If I Ain't Got You*
(Artist)" (Artists) | Won in 2004

Best Female R&B Vocal Performance, *"Fallin'"* | Won in 2001

Best New Artist | Won in 2001

Song of the Year for *"Fallin'"* | Won in 2001

Best R&B Album for *Songs in A Minor* | Won in 2001

Best R&B Song for *"Fallin'"* | Won in 2001

MTV Awards

Best Cinematography for *"Empire State of Mind"*
(Director of Photography: John Perez) | Won in 2010

Best R&B Video for *"Karma"* | Won in 2005

Best R&B Video for *"If I Ain't Got You"* | Won in 2004

Artist to Watch for *"Fallin'"* | Won in 2001

NAACP Image Awards

Outstanding Music Video for *"Girl on Fire"* | Won in 2013

Outstanding Female Artist | Won in 2013

Outstanding Music Video for *"Un-Thinkable (I'm Ready)"* | Won in 2011

Outstanding Album for *"As I Am"* | Won in 2008

Outstanding Music Video for *"Like You'll Never See Me Again"* | Won in 2008

Outstanding Female Artist | Won in 2008

Outstanding Music Video for *"Like You'll Never See Me Again"* | Won in 2008

Outstanding Female Artist | Won in 2008

Outstanding Song for *"Like You'll Never See Me Again"* | Won in 2008

Outstanding Album for *"As I Am"* | Won in 2008

Outstanding Song for *"Unbreakable"* | Won in 2006

Outstanding Music Video for *"Unbreakable"* | Won in 2006

Outstanding Music Video for *"Unbreakable"* | Won in 2006

Outstanding Female Artist | Won in 2006

Outstanding Song for *"Unbreakable"* | Won in 2006

Outstanding Music Video for *"If I Ain't Got You"* | Won in 2005

Outstanding Music Video for *"If I Ain't Got You"* | Won in 2005

Outstanding Song | for *"If I Ain't Got You"* | Won in 2005

Outstanding Female Artist | Won in 2004

Outstanding Song for *"A Woman's Worth"* | Won in 2002

Outstanding Album for *Songs in A minor* | Won in 2002

Outstanding New Artist | Won in 2002

Outstanding Song for *"A Woman's Worth"* | Won in 2002

Alicia Keys HIP-HOP & R&B

Satellite Award

Best Original Song for *"Another Way to Die"* (in Quantum of Solace) | Won in 2008

People's Choice Awards

Favorite R&B Song for "No One" | Won in 2009

Favorite Female Artist | Won in 2005

Soul Train Music Awards

Best R&B/Soul Female Artist | Won in 2010

Best R&B/Soul Single—Group, Band or Duo for *"My Boo"* | Won in 2005

Best R&B/Soul Single, Female for *"If I Ain't Got You"* | Won in 2005

Best R&B/Soul Album, Female for T*he Diary of Alicia Keys* | Won in 2005

Best R&B/Soul Single, Female for *"You Don't Know My Name"* | Won in 2004

Sammy Davis, Jr. Award for Entertainer of the Year (Female) | Won in 2002

Sammy Davis, Jr. for Entertainer of the Year | Won in 2002

Best R&B/Soul or Rap New Artist for *"Fallin'"* | Won in 2002

Best R&B/Soul Album, Female for *Songs in A Minor* | Won in 2002

Soul Train Music Awards

World's Best-Selling R&B Female | Won in 2008

World's Best-Selling R&B Female | Won in 2004

director's research uncovered BlackBerry users' need for a phone that helped them multi-task, complete tasks, and remain active on social networks. Keys left the company the following year.

Success Doesn't Happen Overnight

"Focused," "studious," and "forward-thinking" describe the traits leading to Keys's success. She has continued to devote herself to creative endeavors evolving from a focus on writing for herself to collaboration. She continues to develop a diverse career spanning songwriting, production, acting, and writing. She earned her first acting credit at age four and began studying piano at age seven. She decided that she would succeed, and she poured her efforts into that, getting signed to her first recording contract while in her teens. Now a working mom in her mid-thirties, Alicia Keys continues to develop new projects in a multitude of areas. She's content only when creating, and while she switches gears from project to project, she continues to keep her career moving.

Alicia Keys achieved success through hard work and motivation.

Text-Dependent Questions:

1. With a classmate, discuss Keys's foray into business with BlackBerry. What does a creative director typically do? What education would you typically need to land that job?

2. Why does Keys limit the brands she endorses?

3. What organization has awarded Keys the most accolades?

Research Project:

Research the standard format of a song or rap. Write your own song or rap, developing your rhymes and refrain.

Words to Understand

Payola: A form of bribery in the recording industry, once used to influence radio stations to play certain songs over others.

Quirks: Peculiar or unique behaviors or habits.

Work ethic: An accepted principle stating that hard work deserves reward and is inherently virtuous.

Alicia Keys at the 2016 BET Awards at the Microsoft Theater, Los Angeles.

Alicia Keys HIP-HOP & R&B

Chapter 4

Alicia Keys's Brand Messaging— Becoming a Worldwide Sensation

Alicia Keys's Marketing Strategy

In an industry in which **payola** often influenced airplay, today's artists focus their time and effort on self-promotion. Alicia Keys does much of her own marketing, enhancing the authenticity of her message. Being real sells records. The recording industry still tries to craft and coif its stars, but Keys has avoided that from the beginning. Keys told Oprah "Some people at the label were saying [of her music], 'What's this? It's kind of soulful. Where are the pop smashes?' They wanted my hair blown out and flowing, my dresses shorter. And they wanted me to lose weight."

Keys made the tough decision to leave Columbia Records and move on to Arista, where she quickly ended up moving to the newly formed J Records. She found a label that would allow her to live and create

Alicia Keys has her own distinctive style. She is critical of how some record companies try to craft a star's image.

Alicia Keys

Scan here to watch Alicia Keys's "Girl on Fire" speech at the Women's March on Washington, D.C., on January 21, 2019.

as her authentic self, and a situation where the creative executives wanted her music to sound like her music.

That move opened the door to her unique composition style. It has also allowed her to forge strong relationships with those in the industry with whom she regularly works and with her fans. Keys has a base of fans who remain dedicated to her career whether she brings out a new single or a book or appears in a film. For the fans, Keys has helped bring a new understanding of music and its meaning. She reveals her process and meets with them online to explain lyrics and songs' backstories.

Social Media Tactics

Although she puts years between albums, during her release process Keys begins months ahead of time, working with her marketing and social media staff to create photos, videos, and posts that provide background and insight to the creative process.

For example, when she debuted "Girl on Fire," Keys began three months before the release date. She apprised fans of the release date and album cover then. She debuted a single well in advance of the album's shipping date. She had her social media staff post a steady stream of album-related posts, photos, and videos.

For the release of the album, one week before it shipped, Keys hosted a homemade version of VH-1's *Storytellers*. It had no branding and no TV station behind it. She streamed it for free so all fans could watch it on YouTube and Google+. At this groundbreaking album-introduction, Keys became the first major-label performer to host such an event. She played every song on the album live via the Internet for her fans. After each song, she explained its backstory, its lyrics, and its personal meaning for her.

Keys knew that people often hear a song but cannot understand the lyrics or do not know the larger meaning to them. Lyrics build a connection with the listener, so making sure that they know and understand them can build album sales.

Creativity and Work Ethic

Keys credits her mom's Scotch-Italian roots and upbringing for what gives her a work ethic that gets it done and has enabled her to reach the top. In 2006, she experienced a nervous breakdown, overwhelmed by her newly found fame. She traveled to Egypt to work through what she was feeling. Keys pulled it together admirably, returning to the U.S. to record *As I Am* and return to her slay. Some of her biggest success came after her

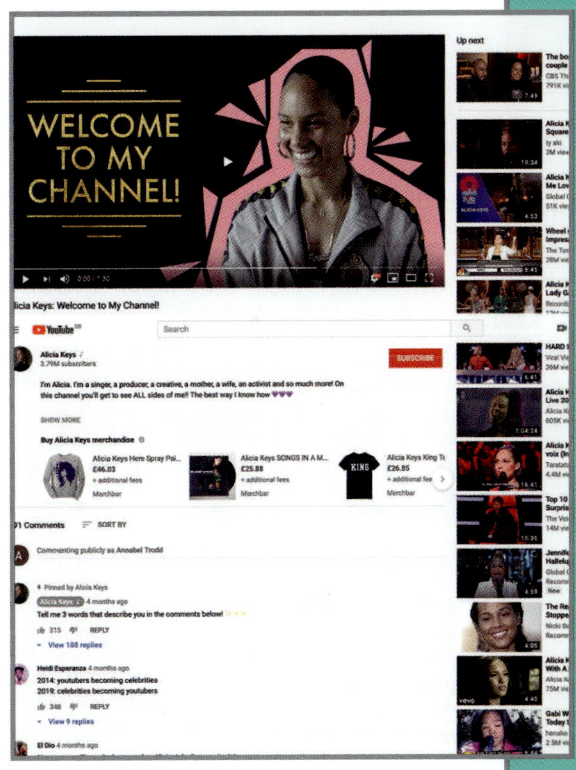

Fans can stream for free on Alicia Keys's YouTube channel.

From an early age, Alicia Keys wasn't afraid to follow her dreams by determination and hard work.

recovery. She continued to eschew drugs and alcohol and has attributed her bounce-back to that persistence.

She held herself accountable. She set goals. She knew she had music inside her to express. She recognized that the business wanted to change her, to make her another Mariah. Alicia Keys recognized she needed to Alicia. Girl from Harlem. Woman with the music career she dreamed of as a little girl. She knew she wanted to marry. She had always dreamed of being a mother.

Determination is key. She decided to recover. "You just have to figure out a balance," Keys told the *Daily Record*. "It couldn't be about work all the time and just going on and on. It was a time when a lot of things needed to be changed, and new things needed to happen in my professional life."

The irony was she did not need to quit music, but to diversify. Keys began focusing more on songwriting with others. She started acting in various projects—short films and features. She guest-starred on numerous television shows. She became a regular on others. She reduced her tour dates and found more projects that let her remain in New York City. She got serious with her old friend Kasseem Dean. Four years after her breakdown, the two married. She also fulfilled her dream of becoming a mother, co-parenting Dean's three children and parenting their two children.

In 2017, with new projects in the mix, she balanced mothering Genesis Ali and Egypt Daoud with work. She also began working on teaching the children how to express themselves appropriately. "I think a lot of times, we're not taught how to express ourselves well, especially boys," she told ABC News.

Her challenge has been to balance the travel her career requires with being a present, active mother. Her eldest child now attends grade school, while the youngest has not yet begun kindergarten. Keys works to provide them consistency. She teaches her children by example. They see her working hard and she communicates her strong **work ethic** to them so they will develop their own. "I trust myself, and I'm glad [Genesis and Egypt] get to see me working hard and going after my dreams so they know what it takes to go after theirs," she told ABC News.

Scan here to listen to Alicia Keys in her collaboration with Drake.

Collaboration and Opportunities at Home and Work

Keys and Dean, who produces under the pseudonym Swizz Beatz, handily share an industry although their positions differ.

Dean has worked as a music producer since his teens, just as Keys has worked as a songwriter since the same age. Longtime friends, they already know one another's **quirks** and work processes. Since they married in 2010, neither has had to travel far to collaborate. The living room or the kitchen can double as an idea hopper. The couple take full advantage of the ability to work together. Their differences compliment their music. For example, Swizz Beatz produced the 1999 hit "Money, Cash, Hoes," and with Keys he produced 2010's "Put It in a Love Song." With Lil Wayne, he produced 2018's "Pistol on My Side (P.O.M.S.)," but with Keys's 2014 "We Are Here."

Study the Greats, and Learn

Keys gets to know new collaborators by sharing her favorite music with them and listening to their favorite music. She studied a variety of music from Mozart and

Alicia Keys has worked as a producer with husband Swizz Beats, working with artists such as Lil Wayne.

Chopin to Nirvana and Curtis Mayfield; Led Zeppelin to Sly and the Family Stone to Satie; Beethoven to Aretha Franklin and Nina Simone; rounded out by Billie Holiday and Ella Fitzgerald. She only listens to music that moves her and reaches her.

Bare Your Soul Carefully

Keys knows that she does not have to share every moment and feeling in her life. She blogs and shares both work aspects and personal life moments. She does not overshare though. She shared the truth of her breakdown in 2006. She also shared the recovery. She did it after the fact, in retrospect, not post by post.

The performer has marshalled her natural honesty and put it to work in her marketing. Rather than trying to reach a target audience, she tries to make a genuine connection to her fans and to those who are going through something similar to what happened to her. Keys simply became a more artful planner and organizer. She has even made room for philanthropy, founding two non-profits.

Alicia Keys enjoys all music genres such as classical, jazz, blues, and rock. She studied the music of Mozart at college.

Alicia Keys

Founding a Non-Profit—In the United States, about 1.56 million non-profits provide services to address the diverse needs of those ranging from diabetic cats homeless veterans to unwed mothers. These organizations raise the revenue they use to serve their population and typically generate it with the help of their boards of directors.

https://www.statista.com/statistics/189245/number-of-non-profit-organizations-in-the-united-states-since-1998/ According to the National Council of Non-Profits, a new non-profit is founded each day to address the social needs of our country.

Persevere

Keys's perseverance paid off when she was looking for a record company. It also paid off when she recovered from her breakdown. Rather than putting off her career, she has continued to create and work on diverse projects after becoming a mother. Her perseverance also paid off through the trouble she had in 2006. She kept a strong focus on her dreams.

Branding the Name Alicia Keys

Keys uses an active social media presence, in-person appearances, speaking engagements, interviews, film and television appearances, and philanthropy to build an authentic brand that reaches each aspect of her life. The honesty with which Alicia Keys lives provides a natural branding that appeals to her fans.

Text-Dependent Questions:

1. Discuss how you think Keys's efforts in promoting "Girl on Fire" succeeded or failed.

2. How does Keys organize and manage her busy schedule?

3. How many children are there in Keys's blended family?

Research Project:

Research the layman's term "nervous breakdown" to gain a better understanding of what Keys went through in 2006. What are some coping mechanisms you could use if your work or home stress were to get out of hand? What coping mechanisms do you see the adults in your household using? How healthy are they?

Words to Understand

Ambassador: An individual who acts as a representative of an activity, organization, or country.

Inauguration: The formal swearing in or assumption of office of an elected official.

Social inequalities: An uneven resource allocation and distribution in society resulting in social castes and problems such as hunger, homelessness, and lack of education.

Alicia Keys wearing suit by Balenciaga attends Billboard's 2018 13th Annual Women in Music gala at Pier 36 in New York City.

Alicia Keys HIP-HOP & R&B

Alicia Keys Reminds Us to Give of Ourselves

Alicia Keys regularly performs at benefit concerts and volunteers as an **ambassador** for children's charities. She supports Frum Tha Ground Up, a youth-oriented non-profit providing academic success tools and scholarships. Keys has recorded tracks to benefit Live 8, a non-profit working to alleviate poverty in Africa. She quickly responds to emergency needs and performed at benefit concerts to aid victims of Hurricane Katrina, Hurricane Sandy, and the Haiti earthquake as well as participating in the Live Earth shows. But Keys also goes far beyond simple volunteering. She has co-founded two charities to help alleviate social justice issues here in the U.S. and in Africa.

Keep a Child Alive

Keys began as an ambassador for Keep a Child Alive but felt so strongly about the work of the non-profit that she stepped in as a co-founder in 2003, donating money for the support

Damage from the 2010 earthquake in Port-au-Prince in Haiti.

and expansion of its goals. She travelled to Kenya, South Africa, and Uganda and met with teenagers and young adults who had lost their parents to AIDS and subsequently had become the heads of their households. "They were so powerful and poetic," Key said of the teens she interviewed. "They wanted to change everything, like, 'This will never be my children.'

The charity provides generic, affordable medicines to the families to fight HIV and AIDS. In addition to the medicines, it provides support to six grassroots organizations in Africa and India that target the socioeconomic roots of the spread of HIV and the development of the AIDS epidemic. The non-profit provides services to more than 70,000 individuals annually. Its overarching goals include preventing new infections, ending barriers to treatment, and ensuring no discrimination to those infected or their families.

To fundraise for the charity, Keys served as musical director for the 2006 Keep a Child Alive Charity Gala. Annually, the charity hosts The Black Ball in New York City to raise funds for the charity. She also donated a private

Singer Usher and Alicia Keys attend the Keep A Child Alive Black Ball in 2010.

concert to its charity auction as a prize. During her trip to Africa, the singer shot a documentary *Alicia in Africa: Journey to the Motherland*, which she released in April of 2008. She also works with Greater Than AIDS on its EMPOWERED campaign, which informs U.S. women about HIV and AIDS.

Keys represented the charity at the 2006 16th International AIDS Conference in Toronto, Canada. In her speech, she drew attention to the needs of children with parents ill with AIDS.

We must come together—individuals, governments, corporations, philanthropists, and artists—as one and fight for the rights of children and families suffering unnecessarily from this dreadful disease. We must never give up until AIDS treatment and realistic prevention messages go hand in hand across the world; until we realize that keeping mothers alive is critical to the well-being of the world's children; and until we can stand together and say, "We did not sit idly by and watch an entire continent perish."

Gender Inequality and the AIDS Epidemic—In sub-Saharan Africa, young women face a five-times-greater likelihood of contracting HIV than young men do. In Africa, women of reproductive age die of AIDS more often than of any other cause of death. In the African areas served by Keep a Child Alive, a young woman is infected with HIV every minute.

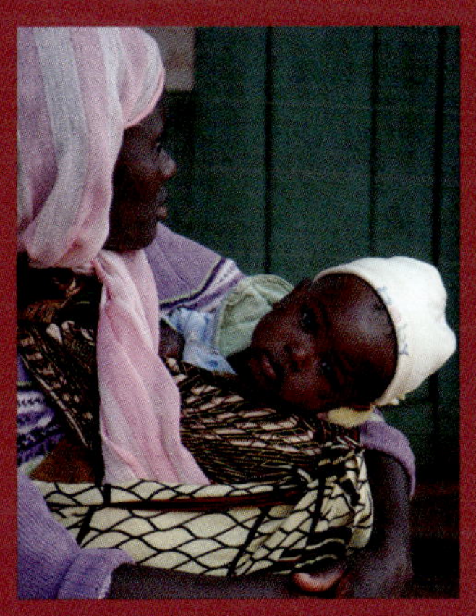

Alicia Keys

Music to Raise Funds and Awareness

Keys and Bono, lead singer of U2, collaborated on a cover of Peter Gabriel and Kate Bush's "Don't Give Up" as a promotional effort for 2005's World AIDS Day. Their version featured Africa in the title and lyrics—"Don't Give Up (Africa)." Keys authored a campaign song for President Obama and performed in the 2007 Nobel Peace Prize Concert in Norway.

ReAct Now: Music and Relief

She joined Bon Jovi, Common, David Banner, Green Day, and U2 at the 4.5-hour September 2005 ReAct televised concert for the Hurricane Katrina survivors. The concert raised about $30 million through the American Red Cross, Feeding America, and the Salvation Army. Keys also appeared on *Shelter from the Storm: A Concert for the Gulf Coast*, a one-hour televised benefit concert.

The aftermath of Hurricane Katrina in New Orleans, Louisiana.

United Nations AID Conference

Keys addressed United Nations representatives at the *HIV Priorities for Positive*

Change: In Women's Words panel at the June 2011 United Nations AID Conference. She served on the panel with musician and philanthropist Annie Lennox. She focused her address on the need for HIV education and universal access for females worldwide.

"If we show the next generation of women and girls that we care by providing the resources to achieve universal access, this will empower them. If we do that, we will stop the epidemic in its tracks," Keys said during the panel.

We Are Here Movement

The singer founded the We Are Here charity to draw attention to the brutal murders of African American men. Her non-profit partnered with MIC to create the video, "23 ways you can be killed if you are black in America." Performers Beyoncé, Janelle Monáe, Pharrell, Rihanna, and Taraji P. Henson joined Keys. The non-profit works with existing charities working on social issues, including OxFam, Girls Rising, The Trayvon Martin Foundation, Partners in Health, and Equal Justice Foundation. Keys funded the non-profit's initial projects with a persona donation of $1 million.

Scan here to listen to the Alicia Keys cover of the classic song "If I Was Your Woman."

Sisters Are Doin' It for Themselves—The original Women's March on Washington, D.C., was meant to be a one-time event initially. It resulted in such a meaningful collaboration among women's groups across the United States that it became a standing annual event. The Women's March developed the Unity Principles to define the diversity of issues they support—ending violence against women, protected reproductive rights, LGBTQIA rights, worker's rights, civil rights, disability and deaf rights, immigrant rights, and environmental justice.

The Women's March on Washington

Keys marched in the Women's March on Washington the day following **inauguration** of President Donald Trump. She stepped up to the mic, not to sing, but to provide a rousing feminist speech, which went viral on the Internet. You can still watch Keys's "Girl on Fire" speech on YouTube. You'll find a link to it in this book. Her call to action included Every Woman, as she marshalled women everywhere to embrace their fire to unleash the potential of women across the world.

"We are mothers, we are caregivers, we are artists, we are activists. We are entrepreneurs, doctors, leaders of industry and technology. Our potential is unlimited. We rise."

Blue Roof Wellness Centre

In Durban, South Africa, Keys designed a health clinic and wellness center that serves those with HIV. The Blue Roof Wellness Centre offers both short- and long-term health facilities, a community

garden, and educational programs. Keys wants to develop a way to scale the facility. She also helped develop Operation Bobbi Bear, a program to help treat sexually abused children, help prevent infection, and aid in their emotional recovery. Children describe what happened to them using a stuffed bear.

Frum Tha Ground Up

Keys also serves as a spokesperson for Frum Tha Ground Up, a non-profit that inspires and motivates American teens to achieve success on all levels. The goal of the organization is to provide youth a foundation for building their own success.

How Alicia Keys Reminds Us to Give Back

As Alicia Keys grew up in Hell's Kitchen, she observed numerous social issues, **social inequalities**, racial issues, and community needs. When she became famous, she began using her success to address the social problems she had observed first hand growing up and in her travels as a musician. She tries hard as a mom to teach her children the same work ethic that brought her success and to live a philanthropic example for them that will rub off.

Alicia uses her high profile to help raise awarness on important issues. Another important aim is for her to be a good role model for others.

Alicia Keys

HIP-HOP & R&B

Text-Dependent Questions:

1. What philanthropic initiative interests you, among those with which Keys volunteers?

2. With which non-profits does Keys work most closely?

3. How could you localize one of the charities with which Keys volunteers?

Research Project:

Keys works to address the inequity in the spread of HIV in the African community, where women are much more likely than average to contract the disease. Research the spread of HIV and AIDS in your community. What sector of society is most likely to contract the disease where you live?

Series Glossary of Key Terms

A&R: an abbreviation that stands for Artists and Repertoire, which is a record company department responsible for the recruitment and development of talent; similar to a talent scout for sports.

ambient: a musical style that relies on electronic sounds, gentle music, and the lack of a regular beat to create a relaxed mood for the listener.

brand: a particular product or a characteristic that serves to identify a particular product; a brand name is one having a well-known and usually highly regarded or marketable word or phrase.

cameo: also called a cameo role; a minor part played by a prominent performer in a single scene of a motion picture or a television show.

choreography: the art of planning and arranging the movements, steps, and patterns of dancers.

collaboration: a product created by working with someone else; combining individual talents.

debut: a first public appearance on a stage, on television, or so on, or the beginning of a profession or career; the first appearance of something, like a new product.

deejay (DJ): a slang term for a person who spins vinyl records on a turntable; aka a disc jockey.

demo: a recording of a new song, or of one performed by an unknown singer or group, distributed to disc jockeys, recording companies, and the like, to demonstrate the merits of the song or performer.

dubbed: something that is named or given a new name or title; in movies, when the actors' voices have been replaced with those of different performers speaking another language; in music, transfer or copying of previously recorded audio material from one medium to another.

endorsement: money earned from a product recommendation, typically by a celebrity, athlete, or other public figure.

entrepreneur: a person who organizes and manages any enterprise, especially a business, usually with considerable initiative and at financial risk.

falsetto: a man singing in an unnaturally high voice, accomplished by creating a vibration at the very edge of the vocal chords.

genre: a subgroup or category within a classification, typically associated with works of art, such as music or literature.

Alicia Keys HIP-HOP & R&B

hone, honing: sharpening or refining a set of skills necessary to achieve success or perform a specific task.

icon: a symbol that represents something, such as a team, a religious person, a location, or an idea.

innovation: the introduction of something new or different; a brand-new feature or upgrade to an existing idea, method, or item.

instrumental: serving as a crucial means, agent, or tool; of, relating to, or done with an instrument or tool.

jingle: a short verse, tune, or slogan used in advertising to make a product easily remembered.

mogul: someone considered to be very important, powerful, and in charge; a term usually associated with heads of businesses in the television, movie studio, or recording industries.

performing arts: skills that require public performance, as acting, singing, or dancing.

philanthropy: goodwill to fellow members of the human race; an active effort to promote human welfare.

public relations: the activity or job of providing information about a particular person or organization to the public so that people will regard that person or organization in a favorable way.

sampler: a digital or electronic musical instrument, related to a synthesizer, that uses samples, or sound recordings, of real instruments (trumpet, violin, piano, etc.) mixed with excerpts of recorded songs and other interesting sounds (sirens, ocean waves, construction noises, car horns, etc.) that are stored digitally and can be replayed by a triggering device, like a sequencer, electronic drums, or a MIDI keyboard.

single: a music recording having two or more tracks that is shorter than an album, EP, or LP; also, a song that is particularly popular, independent of other songs on the same album or by the same artist.

Further Reading

Keys, Alicia. *More Myself: A Journey*. New York: Flatiron Books. 2020.

Tifrere, Mashonda. *Blend: The Secret to Co-Parenting and Creating a Balanced Family*. New York: Penguin. Penguin Audio. 2018.

Internet Resources

www.billboard.com
The official site of Billboard Music, with articles about artists, chart information, and more.

www.thefader.com
Official website for a popular New York City–based music magazine.

www.hiphopweekly.com
A young-adult hip-hop magazine.

www.thesource.com
Website for a bi-monthly magazine that covers hip-hop and pop culture.

www.vibe.com
Music and entertainment website and a member of Billboard Music, a division of Billboard-Hollywood Reporter Media Group.

https://www.instagram.com/aliciakeys
Alicia Keys's official Instagram for all the latest photos.

https://twitter.com/aliciakeys
Alicia Keys's official Twitter for all the latest news and updates.

https://www.facebook.com/aliciakeys
Alicia Keys's official Facebook page for all the latest news and updates.

http://aliciakeys.com
Alicia Keys's official website—the go-to source for all official updates and music.

Citations

"Alicia Keys—Time Machine." The Culture Curators. November 18, 2019.
https://theculturecurators.com/alicia-keys-time-machine/

"Watch: Alicia Keys VH1 Storytellers (Full Video)." Vibe. November 13, 2012.
https://www.vibe.com/2012/11/watch-alicia-keys-vh1-storytellers-full-video

"Drake on Working with Alicia Keys." Rap Radar. December 8, 2009.
https://rapradar.com/2009/12/08/drake-on-working-with-alicia-keys/

"V Exclusive: Nas Talks About Performing with Jay-Z and Alicia Keys at Carnegie Hall." Vibe. April 26, 2012.
https://www.vibe.com/2012/04/v-exclusive-nas-talks-about-performing-jay-z-and-alicia-keys-carnegie-hall

"Aretha Franklin Talks Beyonce, Alicia Keys and Jennifer Hudson: 'I Hear My Influence.'" Billboard. November 7, 2014.

https://www.billboard.com/articles/news/6311841/aretha-franklin-on-beyonce-jennifer-hudson-alicia-keys-new-album

Mossman, Kate. "Alicia Keys: 'I want to make sure all the issues about race are addressed.'" The Guardian. November 06, 2016.

https://amp.theguardian.com/music/2016/nov/04/alicia-keys-i-want-to-make-sure-all-issues-race-hillary-clinton-here-interview

"National Youth Gang Survey Analysis: Measuring the Extent of Gang Problems." National Gang Center. Accessed December 06, 2019.

https://www.nationalgangcenter.gov/survey-analysis/measuring-the-extent-of-gang-problems

"Echo Awards. Awards and Winners." Accessed December 6, 2019.
http://www.awardsandwinners.com/category/echo-awards/

"Alicia Keys protests tobacco sponsorship." Hollywood Reporter. July 31, 2008.
https://www.hollywoodreporter.com/news/alicia-keys-protests-tobacco-sponsorship-116654

Ismail, Noreem. "Levi's snags Alicia Keys for its latest campaign." [VIDEO]. Marketing Interactive. September 7, 2015.
https://www.marketing-interactive.com/levis-snags-alicia-keys-latest-campaign-video/

"Levi's Partners with Alicia Keys to Launch an All New Women's Jean Collection." July 9, 2015.
https://brandingforum.org/news/levis-partners-with-alicia-keys-to-launch-an-all-new-womens-jean-collection/

Tahmincioglu, Eve. "More women holding down multiple jobs." NBC News. March 21, 2015.
http://www.nbcnews.com/id/35912763/ns/business-careers/t/more-women-holding-down-multiple-jobs/#.Xew-gJ5MF0t

Srisavasdi, Rachanee. "Blackberry: Alicia Keys to the rescue?" Global Marketing Professor. February 24, 2013
https://globalmarketingprofessor.com/blackberry-z10-alicia-keys-to-the-rescue/

"BlackBerry and singer Alicia Keys Part Ways." The Verge. February 24, 2013.
https://www.theverge.com/2014/1/2/5266838/blackberry-and-singer-alicia-keys-part-ways"Scots roots instilled a work
ethic that helped make me successful, says U.S. singer Alicia Keys." The Daily Record. December 6, 2019.
https://www.dailyrecord.co.uk/entertainment/celebrity/scots-roots-instilled-a-work-ethic-1053603

"Alicia Keys talks teaching sons how to express their emotions, develop work ethic." ABC News. May 5, 2017.
https://abcnews.go.com/Entertainment/alicia-keys-talks-teaching-sons-express-emotions-develop/story?id=47230779

"How to Start a Nonprofit." Council for Non-Profits. Accessed December 6, 2019.
https://www.councilofnonprofits.org/tools-resources/how-start-nonprofit

"Alicia Keys Charity Work, Events and Causes. Look to the Stars." Accessed December 6, 2019.
https://www.looktothestars.org/celebrity/alicia-keys

"Alicia Keys. Philanthropic People." Accessed December 6, 2019.
https://www.philanthropicpeople.com/profiles/alicia-keys/

"Meet our Co-Founder. Keep a Child Alive." Accessed December 6, 2019.
http://keepachildalive.org/about-us/alicia-keys/

"Alicia Keys on why she started her organization 'We Are Here.'" Fushion. Accessed December 6, 2019.
https://fusion.tv/video/19032/alicia-keys-on-why-she-started-her-organization-we-are-here/

Alicia Keys's Five Most Philanthropic Moments. I Am Megan Ambers (Blog). Accessed December 6, 2019.
https://iammeganambers.com/2017/01/25/alicia-keys-five-most-philanthropic-moments/amp/

"A Trip to South Africa Gave Alicia Keys 'a New Purpose' to Launch Keep a Child Alive." Variety. April 10, 2018.
https://variety.com/2018/music/news/alicia-keys-keep-a-child-alive-africa-1202747999/amp/

"About Us." Women's March. Accessed December 5, 2019.
https://womensmarch.com/mission-and-principles

Educational Video Links

Chapter 1:

http://x-qr.net/1J4P
http://x-qr.net/1JrL
http://x-qr.net/1KiQ
http://x-qr.net/1Jd9
http://x-qr.net/1KyP
http://x-qr.net/1MAC
http://x-qr.net/1Kcf

Chapter 2:

http://x-qr.net/1L9u

Chapter 3:

http://x-qr.net/1M3m

Chapter 4:

http://x-qr.net/1KEe
http://x-qr.net/1LXt
http://x-qr.net/1JuX

Chapter 5:

http://x-qr.net/1Kj6

Alicia Keys
HIP-HOP & R&B

Index

Picture Credits

Chapter 1:

Featureflash Photo Agency | Dreamstime.com
Michael Bush | Dreamstime.com
Everett Collection | Shutterstock.com
Carrienelson | Dreamstime.com
Carrienelson | Dreamstime.com
Michael Bush | Dreamstime.com
Debby Wong | Shutterstock.com
Debby Wong | Shutterstock.com
J Stone | Shutterstock.com
Featureflash Photo Agency/Paul Smith |
  Shutterstock.com
Tinseltown | Shutterstock.com
DFree | Shutterstock.com
Adam J. Sablich | Shutterstock.com
Fabio Diena | Shutterstock.com

Chapter 2:

Fabio Diena | Shutterstock.com
DFree | Shutterstock.com
Eric Landonien | Shutterstock.com
Fabio Diena | Shutterstock.com
Featureflash Photo Agency | Shutterstock.com
VIIIPhotography | Shutterstock.com
Kathy Hutchins | Shutterstock.com
J Stone | Shutterstock.com
FashionStock.com | Shutterstock.com
Tinseltown | Shutterstock.com

Chapter 3:

Starstock | Dreamstime.com
ph.FAB | Shutterstock.com
Wikimedia Commons | Fair Use
Tinseltown | Shutterstock.com
Tinseltown | Shutterstock.com
S_Buckley | Dreamstime.com

Chapter 4:

Featureflash Photo Agency | Shutterstock.com
Featureflash Photo Agency | Shutterstock.com
Kyle Besler | Shutterstock.com
Everett Historican | Shutterstock.com

Chapter 5:

Lev Radin | Shutterstock.com
arindambanerjee | Shutterstock.com
Debby Wong | Shutterstock.com
Franco Volpato | Shutterstock.com
Brian Nolan | Shutterstock.com
Kathy Hutchins | Shutterstock.com
Kathy Hutchins | Shutterstock.com
J Stone | Shutterstock.com
Antonio Scorza
NeelSky | Shutterstock.com
Casimiro | Shutterstock.com
Tinsletown | Shutterstock.com
Jaguar PS | Shutterstock.com
Fabio Diena | Shutterstock.com

Front cover:

Tinseltown | Shutterstock.com

Video Credits

http://x-qr.net/1J4P/Alicia Keys
http://x-qr.net/1JrL/Alicia Keys
http://x-qr.net/1KiQ/Alicia Keys
http://x-qr.net/1Jd9/Alicia Keys
http://x-qr.net/1KyP/Alicia Keys
http://x-qr.net/1MAC/ Billboard
http://x-qr.net/1Kcf/Alicia Keys
http://x-qr.net/1L9u/Alicia Keys
http://x-qr.net/1M3m/Alicia Keys
http://x-qr.net/1KEe/The Hollywood Reporter
http://x-qr.net/1LXt /USA News Live
http://x-qr.net/1JuX/Precious A
http://x-qr.net/1Kj6/Marie P

Author's Biography

Carlie Lawson began writing professionally in 1991. She spent five years at a mid-sized daily newspaper, beating deadline on a daily basis while covering politics and entertainment. She has written for monthly magazines, weekly blogs, and academic publications. Educated at the University of Oklahoma, Carlie holds Bachelor's degrees in Journalism & Mass Communication, and in Film & Video Studies as well as a Master of Regional & City Planning. Carlie owns a consulting firm and conducts research in the area of natural and environmental planning. She also owns a public relations firm. She enjoys hiking, travel, reading, music, guitar, her cat, and the positive-thinking process. Learn more at https://www.writeraccess.com/writer/13038/.

Alicia Keys

HIP-HOP & R&B